From Lava to LIFE

Book Two

The Universe Tells Our Earth Story

By Jennifer Morgan

Illustrated by Dana Lynne Andersen

Dawn Publications

Dedications

To the children of all Earthlings. – JM

To my daughter Rachel, who is living proof that the universe
conspires toward truth, goodness and beauty. In her wisdom and
kindness I am sheltered. May the glory and beauty of Creation sing
in all Souls. May the "one song" of the "uni-verse" resound. — DLA

Illustrations for this book were generously supported by a grant from the Infinity Foundation.

Photographs on pages 2, 3, 41, 42 and 43 courtesy of David Denning and Bruce Russell,
copyright BioMEDIA Associates (www.ebiomedia.com) except the photograph of the opossum
on page 43, by Travis Gale.

Copyright © 2003 Jennifer Morgan
Illustrations copyright © 2003 Dana Lynne Andersen

A Sharing Nature With Children Book

Library of Congress Cataloging-in-Publication Data

Morgan, Jennifer, 1955-
    From lava to life : the universe tells our earth story / by Jennifer Morgan ; illustrated by
Dana Lynne Andersen. — 1st ed.
       p. cm. — (A sharing nature with children book)
    Continues the author's Born with a bang.
    Summary: A history of the Earth, from its formation through the appearance of mammals
and the extinction of dinosaurs, in the form of a story told by the Universe itself to an
Earthling.
    Includes bibliographical references (p. 46).
    ISBN 1-58469-043-7 (hardback) — ISBN 1-58469-042-9 (pbk.)
    1. Life—Origin—Juvenile literature. 2. Earth—History—Juvenile literature.
[1. Earth—History.]   I. Andersen, Dana Lynne, ill. II. Title. III. Series.
   QH325.M773 2003
   576.8'3—dc21   2002015114

*The photograph on this and
the opposing page shows a
type of spherical clumping
bacteria that live all over—in
soil, air, water, and on skin.*

Dawn Publications
P.O. Box 2010
Nevada City, CA 95959
530-478-0111
nature@dawnpub.com
www.dawnpub.com

Printed in Korea

10 9 8 7 6 5 4 3 2 1
First Edition
Design and computer production by Andrea

My Dearest Earthling,

It's so good to share with you the next part of my story. If you haven't heard the first part, you may not know me. I am the Uni-verse. I am everything. Really. Everything. I am all the gleaming galaxies, the whole Earth, every rock, every flea on every cat. You don't have to look far to find me because I am you too. You have always been part of me.

In my first story, I told you how I was born about 13 billion years ago as a tiny speck with a wild and dazzling dream. My dream was so powerful I exploded and grew bigger and bigger. Over a long time, I turned into zillions of galaxies. At the end of the first part of my story, your planet Earth had just been born.

So . . . settle in with your favorite pillow and I'll tell you how rivers of lava turned into rowdy reptiles and flashy flowers. Imagine a time, five billion years ago . . .

Inside a huge spinning disk of dust, Earth began as a pint-sized planetary pup, warmed by the Sun. But she couldn't stay small.

For millions of years, meteors crashed into Earth. Each one made her grow bigger and hotter.

She began to melt and turn herself inside out, over and over. Her sizzling red lava spewed into vast glowing seas.

It's a good thing you weren't human back then. You would have burned to a crisp in a flash. But you *were* there—as particles of stardust, churning inside Earth's oceans of liquid rock.

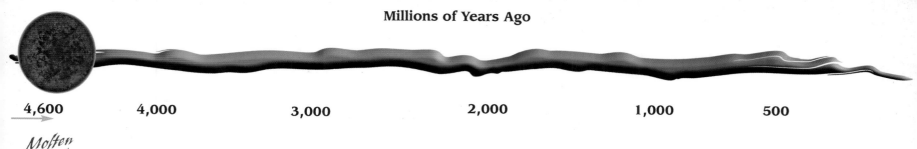

Earth was one of my most imaginative young planets.

Her dreams were packed with worms and wolves, daffodils and dinos, raccoons and baboons, peach trees and palm trees, caves and castles.

Would Earth become all those things in her dreams?

I wondered too, would Earth become—

lilies with lips or
trekking trees with knobby knees?

How I loved your special planet. Earth and other planets like her, sprinkled through all my galaxies, had dreams of coming alive.

4,600   **4,000**   **3,000**   **2,000**   **1,000**   **500**

Molten Earth

Meteors finally stopped bombing Earth. She cooled and her crust hardened. Steamy clouds cooled too, and condensed into drops of water. It was a glorious moment when the Great Rain began! It poured for millions of years, until oceans covered your Earth.

Molten red rocks pushed up through cracks in the ocean floor.

Lightning bolts zapped the seas. Rock, water and air crunched and crashed. Bits of carbon—made inside of stars—hooked together into long chains that folded and looped into tiny slippery bubbles. And then the most amazing thing happened.

The teensy bubbles began to twist and turn, not only when waves crashed or lightning flashed—but on their own! Earth was alive!

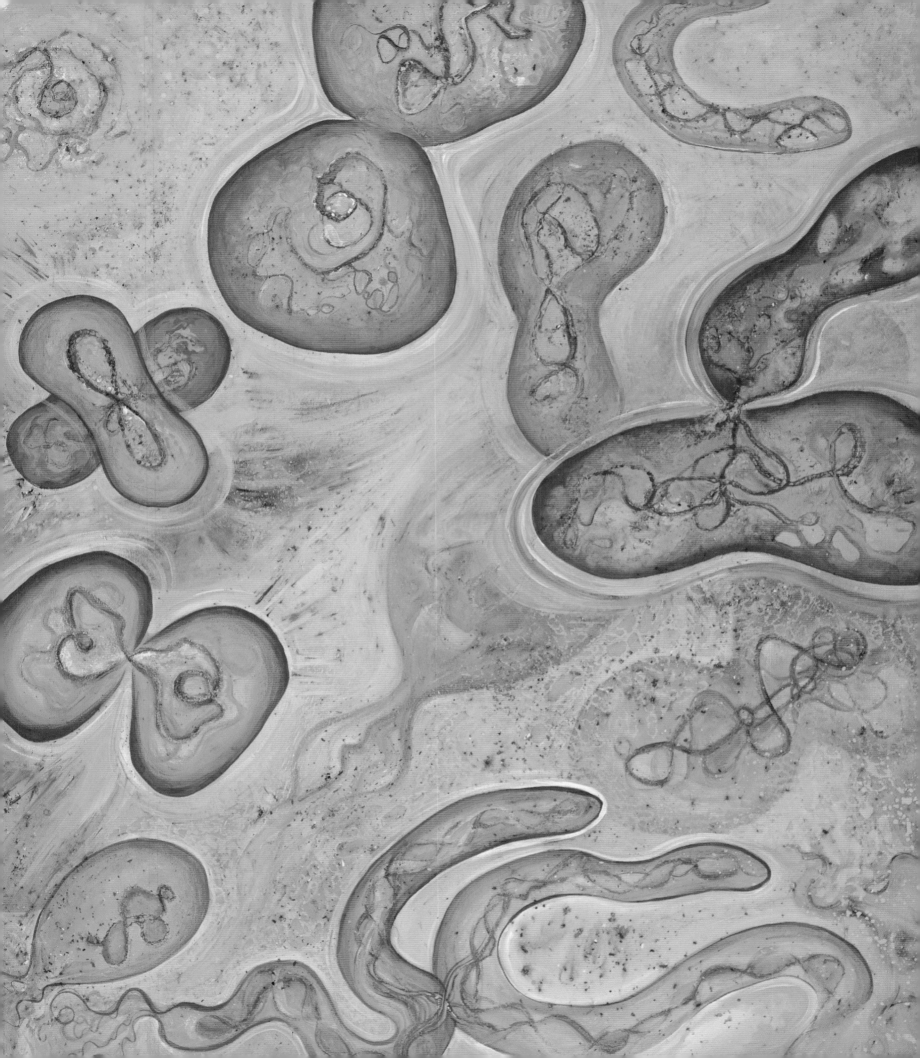

4,600   4,000   3,000   2,000   1,000   500

Molten   Bacteria
Earth

That ancient living stew brought forth the very first Earthlings. They were BACTERIA.

Even now, invisible bacteria are the living nuts and bolts of all life. Millions are in every breath you take. Billions are in every handful of soil. Billions more live and work inside you. Right now, they are helping to digest your breakfast. Oh yes, some can make you sick, but lots more give you life. In fact, you human Earthlings might well say, "Bacteria R Us" and thank them once in awhile!

Right from the start, 4,000 million years ago, bacteria were hungry. Their food was hydrogen. Remember hydrogen? The very first element I created? Bacteria ate it right out of gas bubbles gurgling up from cracks in the ocean floor. The ones who couldn't eat hydrogen, perished. Those who could, lived and split apart into more bacteria.

They passed on their special knowledge through invisible chains of carbon called DNA.

DNA is a code that stores information. Bacteria can rub up against each other and one can even give its DNA to the other. That's how they pass around information about the latest techniques for chowing down on hydrogen. In case you haven't noticed, I have a special fondness for bacteria.

Science Concept: The Rise of Bacteria (see page 41)

| 4,600 | 4,000 | 3,000 | 2,000 | 1,000 | 500 |

Molten Earth   *Bacteria*

For bacteria, absorbing new information about diets and lifestyles was a cinch. You could say they were fast learners. Some learned to eat iron. Some set up shop on the mouths of fiery volcanoes; others journeyed to polar ice caps. Wherever bacteria went, they traded information through their global network, the very first world wide web.

Everywhere, mounds of bacteria—cities really—rose in shallow ocean waters. Bacteria on top ate rays of light and magically transformed sun energy into food.

What wizards they were!

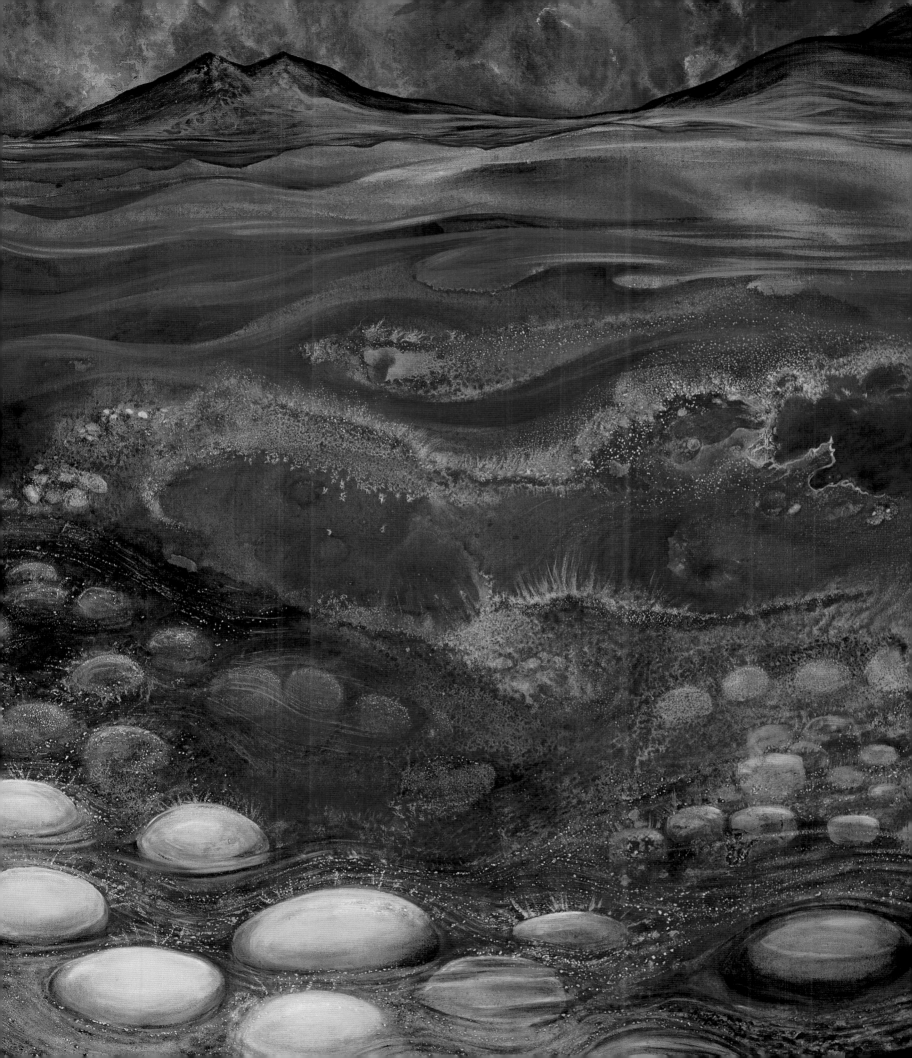

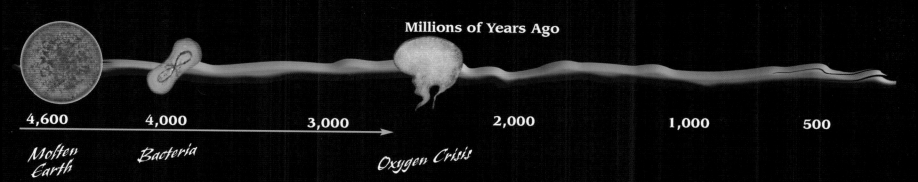

Even though they could snack on sunlight, iron, and other tasty things, *all* bacteria needed their daily dinner of hydrogen. Hungry bacteria fanned out through the seas, and even on land, in search of new hydrogen hunting grounds. Then they discovered that hydrogen was all around them! Water is made out of hydrogen and oxygen.

The sunlight-eating wizards used sun energy to pry hydrogen away from oxygen in water. Then they gobbled up the hydrogen

Their H_2O-busting technology turned Earth's oceans into a resource bonanza! Wow—I was so proud of them!

But their discovery had a dark side. *Once free, oxygen was a deadly poison to bacteria.*

As bacteria busily busted apart H_2O, oxygen gas whooshed out of the oceans and into Earth's atmosphere. The bacteria wizards created their own pollution crisis. Bacteria began to die. Earth was sick. She was in the midst of her first great extinction. Was Earth going to die?

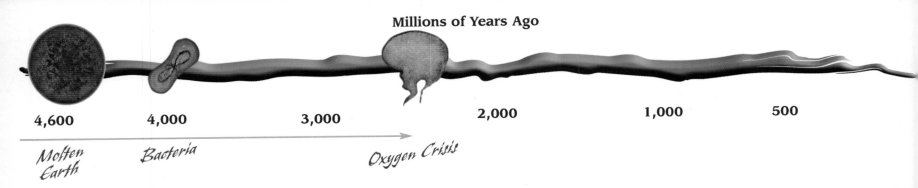

Things got worse.
Hungry bacteria began
to eat each other!

Predators liquefied their prey, then drank them. What a gross, gooey mess! Big bacteria devoured small bacteria. Feisty little bacteria were equally fierce. They burrowed *inside* big bacteria and liquefied their guts from the inside. Sometimes little ones multiplied inside big ones until there were so many little ones that the big ones exploded. Eeeewww!

I realized that a whole new kind of life had just come into being. They were life-eaters.

They could only survive by eating other living things. The sunlight-eaters weren't eating each other. They didn't need to. Their energy came from sunlight, air, water and rock. I'm sure I don't have to tell you whether you're a sunlight-eater or a life-eater.

Eating one's neighbor was more than rude. One part of me was killing another part of me. What good could possibly come of this mess? I did not know.

16 Science Concept: Predators begin to prowl (see page 42)

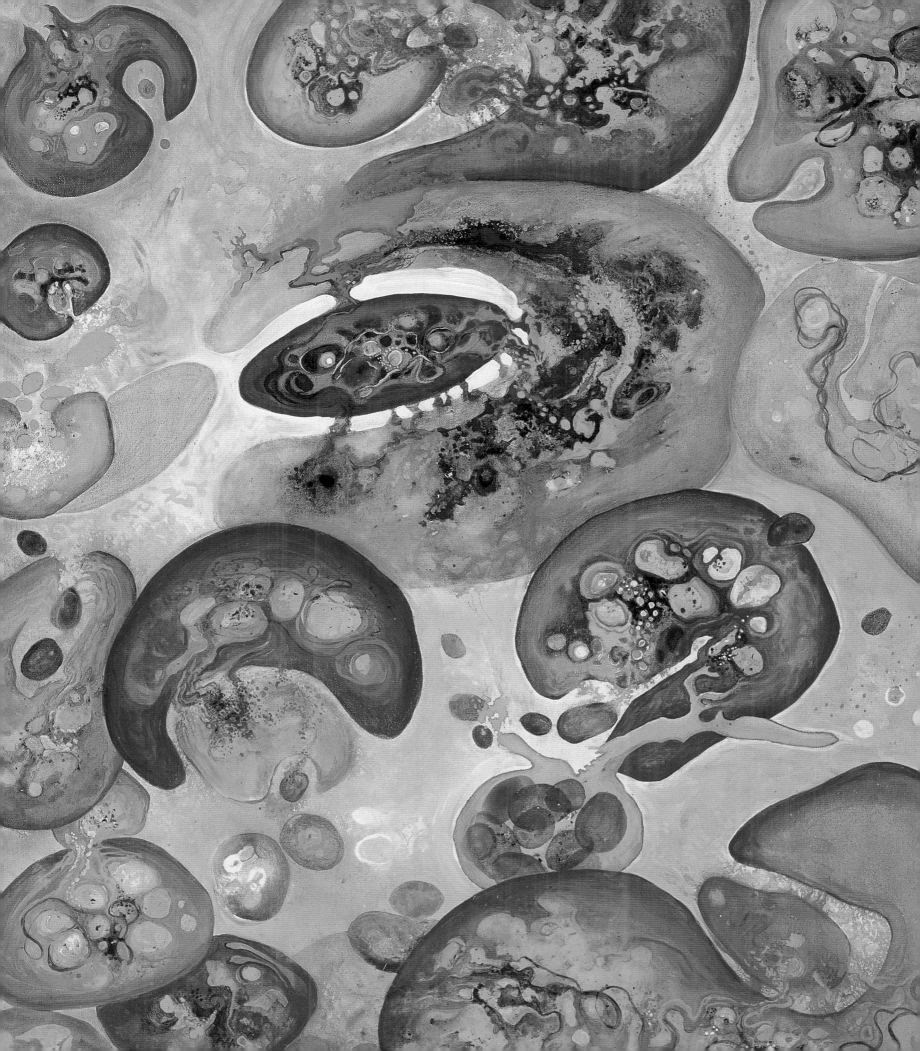

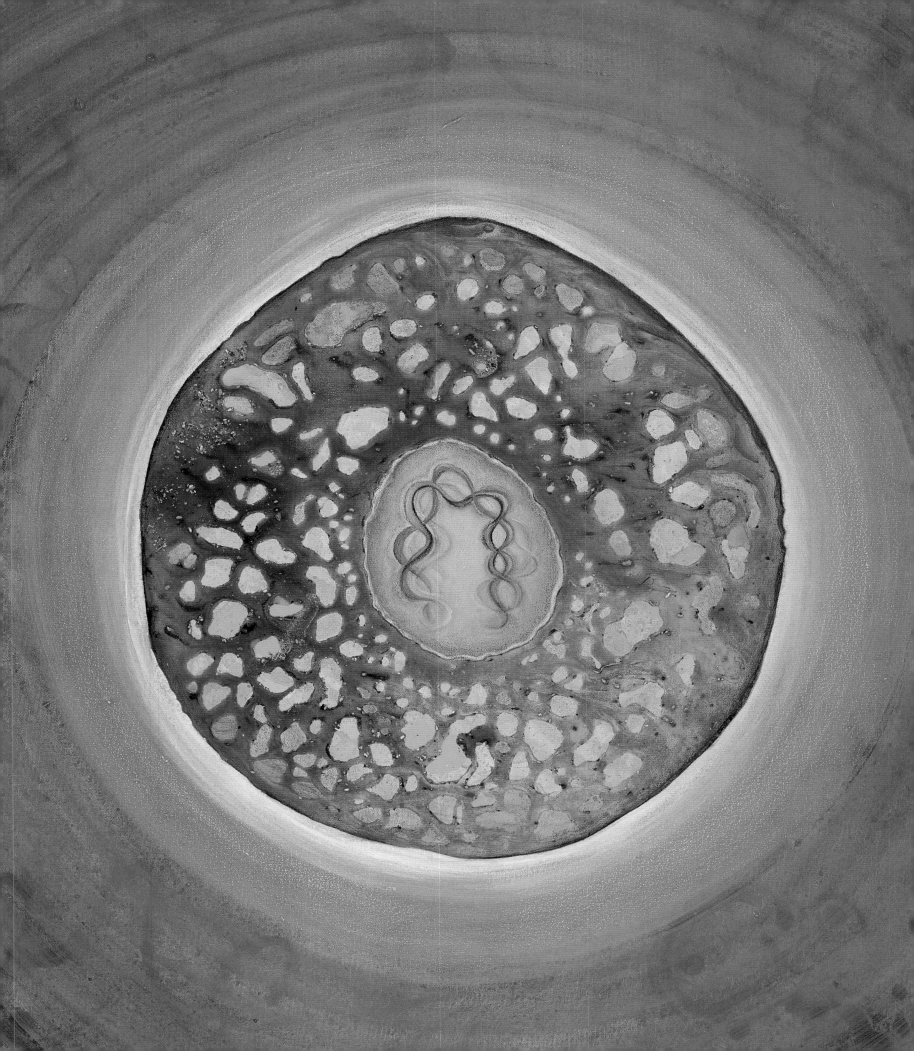

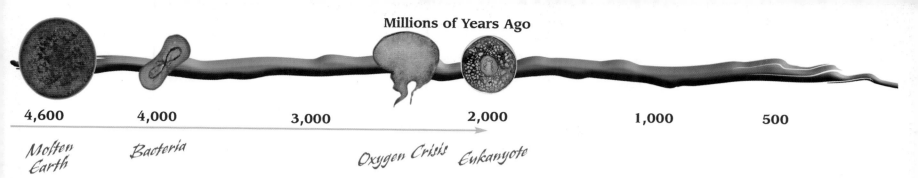

In the midst of all this mayhem, about 2,000 million years ago, something incredible happened. It might have been accidental, but I don't think so.

Two battling bacteria tried to turn each other into a liquid lunch. Instead, they merged into a new Earthling— a EUKARYOTE (you-CARRY-oat).

But rather than let its DNA float loosely around the entire cell, as bacteria do, this new being stashed its DNA inside a protective packet called a *nucleus.* Having a nucleus as a control center made eukaryotes very different from bacteria.

Meanwhile, poisonous oxygen clouds kept closing in.

Eukaryotes had many new talents, but coping with oxygen was not one of them. Earth's disaster was turning into a mega-disaster, far worse than anything humans have ever seen. Something had to happen!

Science Concept: Eukaryotes pack DNA into a nucleus (see page 42)

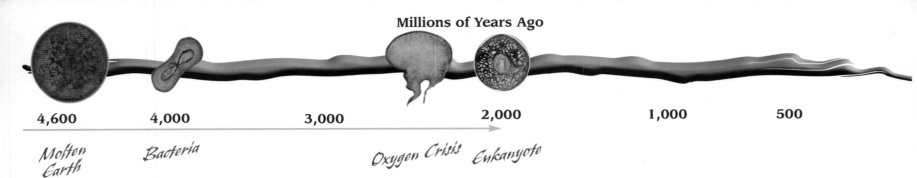
Earth's oceans were filled with zillions of dying eukaryotes and bacteria.

Then, a whipper-snapper of a bacteria turned oxygen poison into power. Who were these tiny powerhouses? MITOCHONDRIA.

At first, eukaryotes and mitochondria were fierce enemies, always turning each other into delectable gooey meals. Then something very strange happened.

To escape predators, mitochondria hid inside eukaryotes. They mopped up the oxygen poison and made energy for them both.

In exchange, eukaryotes protected mitochondria from predators. Now that's an awesome partnership! Mitochondria, once free-living bacteria, live inside all plants and animals, even you. Every second, your mitochondria engines are burning oxygen to power you. It's true, bacteria created your oxygen atmosphere and they breathe oxygen for you. Do you see why I love them so much?

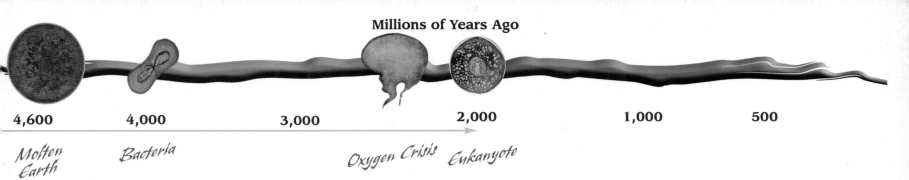

Life mixed and morphed in the soupy, salty sea. At first, eukaryotes reproduced themselves the way bacteria do—they just split apart and kept on rolling.

Then two snuggly eukaryotes paired off and *fused* into one entirely new being.

It was the beginning of sexual reproduction. It meant that the new eukaryotes looked or behaved a little differently from either parent cell. Ah, what complexity that innovation made possible. It boggles the mind.

Those eukaryotes were a social bunch. Most discovered it was easier to live in teams, or colonies, rather than alone.

About 700 million years ago, some teams began to look like large thick fingerprints slowly sliding over rocks and sand. All of them had soft mushy bodies. Bones, shells, jaws, and teeth—all hard body parts—were inventions of the distant future.

Inside each colony, every eukaryote had a special job. Some took in food. Others handled garbage patrol. Oh how I marveled at their incredible teamwork. Still, I wondered how could life evolve from soft gushy beings into pansies, penguins and policemen?

Some brand new colonies became the very first ANIMALS. Wow!

These eukaryote colonies ate living things. Each began as a single cell that grew to have billions of tightly connected cells. They were soft and blobby. Through some great mystery, most of these Earthlings disappeared. Then about 540 million years ago, there was an amazing change.

Earth's animal population began to explode, and to morph into dazzling body designs.

Squishy *jellyfish* twitched their long stringy tentacles and developed the very first muscles.

Tough *trilobites* led the way in making hard things, like a skeleton shield. That's not all: They invented the very first eyes, made out of clear crystals.

Wiggly *worms* began to build the beginnings of brains and backbones. Guess what? They really were your ancestors.

The awesome *Opabinia* had five mushroom-shaped eyes on top of its head and used a long, clawed vacuum nozzle to snatch its prey.

Everywhere, brand new animals were beginning to move, see, and think in more and more complicated ways. It was very exciting!

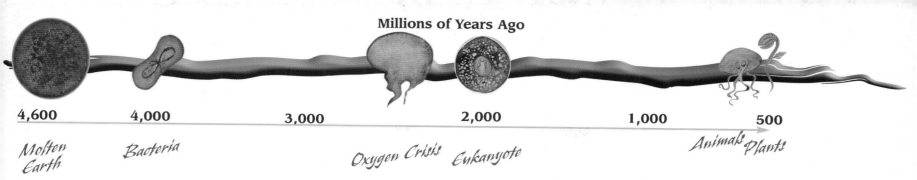

About 500 million years ago, as ocean tides went out each day, two different groups of eukaryotes got stuck on shore.

One eukaryote group ate sunlight. The other ate soil. They found each other and became the very first PLANTS and FUNGI.

You might say they fell in love because you always find them together, trading Sun and Earth energy. Their marriage changed Earth forever. Moss and giant ferns began to spread with their fungi partners underground. Some ferns grew into giant fern trees.

Animals with a hard outside came out of the sea and took to the air. They became—INSECTS. Gargantuan dragonflies with wingspans as wide as seagulls' zig-zagged along the shore.

Somehow a few fish turned their fins into stubby web-like feet. The lure of land was so great that their fish gills began to change into air-breathing lungs. It took millions of years for land and water to shape your ancestors into an entirely new kind of animal that lived both on land and in water. But it happened. They were—AMPHIBIANS!

Your amphibian ancestors had to lay their eggs in water.

A brand new egg appeared on land. It had a leathery shell so the embryo wouldn't dry out.

What's more, these eggs packed a box lunch—a nice juicy yellow yolk, to feed the growing embryo until it was ready to hatch.

Who laid these extra strength, highly fortified eggs? REPTILES!

Now they could explore the continents. Meanwhile, the continents were slowly moving about. They were separate for a long time. Then they slid toward each other and collided into one giant landmass called Pangaea. Reptiles easily spread everywhere.

Then around 245 million years ago, something happened that killed almost all life, in Earth's greatest mass extinction ever. Most amphibians and reptiles perished. Among the dead were those precious Earthlings who invented eyes, trilobites. Every single one disappeared forever. Why was so much life stamped out? It's a great mystery.

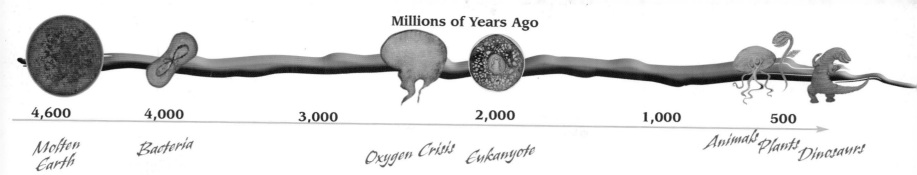

Thankfully, some reptiles did survive. Before long, they tried out new crawling techniques. Lizard reptiles splayed their legs out to the side, twisting their bodies as they crawled over rocks. Two groups of reptiles grew legs that went straight down below their bodies. At first both groups were pretty similar. But little changes—a slight change in skull design here, an adjustment in tooth design there—eventually led to huge differences.

One group of reptiles turned into raucous rulers. They were DINOSAURS.

Dinosaurs celebrated life to the max! Some long-necked plant-eating dinosaurs like *Seismosaurus*, the "Earthquake Lizard," were longer than half a football field and heavier than 1,000 people. There were cute chicken-sized dinosaurs too, who could tear apart lizards with their tiny jaws. And there were large flesh eaters, like *Allosaurus*, and its later relative, the greatest flesh-cruncher of them all, *Tyrannosaurus rex*.

The other group of reptiles turned into fuzzy, mousy animals less than five inches long. They were MAMMALS!

Some were destined to be your great, great—a million times great—grandparents. For 150 million years, the dazzling dinosaurs hardly noticed them scurrying about underfoot and nursing their young under bushes.

Science Concept: Out of reptiles—dinosaurs and mammals (see page 43)

Huge flying reptiles with wings of skin ruled the skies. Then a ferocious little dinosaur morphed and morphed. Over countless generations, its scales turned into feathers and its tiny arms turned into soaring wings with claws.

Some dinosaurs became BIRDS!

Animals depended on plants to make food for them. Plants needed animals to spread their kind to new places.

Plants and animals struck a deal. Plants made yummy nectar, fruits and seeds; and animals carried pollen and seeds far and wide.

The seeds grew into food that animals ate and carried further, where the seeds grew into food that animals ate and carried further, where the seeds grew into food that animals ate and carried still further, where . . . you get the idea. Plants and animals began to depend on each other so much that one would die without the other. That's why, over a long time, plants began to grow splashy, fragrant flowers, their way of shouting, "Dinner's ready! Come and get it!" Magnolia flowers served up suppers on pearly petals. What a feast for hungry beetles!

But in the midst of beauty and light, sixty-five million years ago, a great darkness was about to descend.

It started as any other day. A bird chirped in a Magnolia tree. Ferns ate sunlight. A family of mini-mammals munched on beetles. Dinosaurs began to stir.

High above, a huge meteor, six miles wide, hurtled through space, then plunged toward Earth at 40,000 miles per hour. Oh, no!

It slammed into Earth near what is now Mexico. Like a cannonball, it punched a hole so deep in her crust that Earth's molten insides erupted all over the planet, through volcanoes and cracks in the ocean floor, even on the other side of the planet, in what is now India. It was as if a mega-nuclear bomb had hit. Huge rocks and dust exploded into the atmosphere. Tidal waves drowned all life near shores. Forest fires burned across the globe. Some rocks even vaporized in the searing heat.

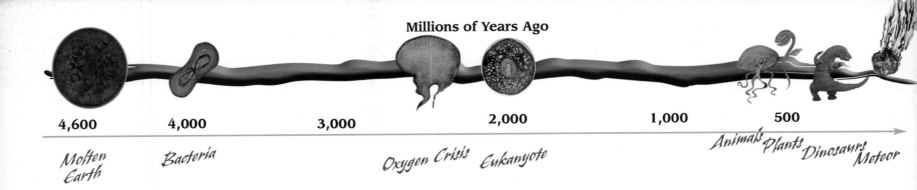

Sunlight couldn't penetrate the sooty veil that blanketed Earth. Without sunlight, plants began to die, and that triggered a cascade of death as species after species were knocked down like dominoes. Plant-eaters fell, then flesh-eaters died. Without animals to carry pollen and seeds, even more plants died.

When the fires finally cooled, Earth cooled too, and went into a deep freeze. Almost all Earthlings in the sea died and most large land animals perished.

Every single dinosaur sank into the dark night of extinction.

Who could carry my story forward now? Could I depend on those few scraggly birds still flitting about? Or those scrubby mini-mammals, huddling together for warmth and gnawing bits of frozen flesh off dead dinosaurs?

There was Earth, once again, smack in the middle of another disaster.

What would happen to Earth's dragonflies, her flying beetles? How would *you* ever be born? Earth had been through so many poisonings and poundings.

But Earth's imagination wouldn't quit. A lot more is still to come.

Bats, woolly mammoths, dolphins, and those remarkable humans, will appear. Human mammals will stand up, cook food over fires, dig for dinosaur bones, and tell great fairy tales. And it will all happen over only 65 million years. That's just a tiny sliver of Earth's entire life story—less than two percent, if you want to get mathematical about it.

But that story will have to wait for another day. Until then, never forget that *you* are *me*—the Universe—being *you*. Till we talk again, hold me in your thoughts, my special one. I think of you always.

Love,

Your Universe

P.S. You can see that I learned a lot through Earth's adventure, which was my adventure too, of course. You may have learned some of these things too.

I learned . . .

○ that everything starts as a dream.

○ that I can make a lot of things out of hydrogen.

○ that I love morphing into new things.

○ that when I'm in crisis, I get creative.

○ that differences, though little at first, can become enormous.

○ that enemies can become partners.

○ that mutants propel my story.

○ that I love putting Earthlings inside of Earthlings.

○ that big surprises can crash in and change everything.

○ that life, food and surroundings mold each other.

○ that one kind of life can "rule" and then perish.

○ that Earthlings have to give and receive energy, or they die.

○ that my adventure depends on all of my parts living their own adventures.

By the way, did you notice that I left lots of fossil clues around for Earthling scientists to piece together my story? Pretty neat, isn't it?

A Timeline of Triumphs in the Earth's Life

The Hadeon Eon—Before Life: 4,600 to 4,000 million years ago

Millions of Years Ago

4,600   4,000   3,000   2,000   1,000   500

Molten Earth

4,600 mya: Earth is born of meteors. A disk made of dust and gas began to spin and condense. The center became superheated and flared into a new star, our Sun. In the outer parts of the disk, particles smashed into each other and formed "planetesimals," or small planets. Meteor bombardment caused these small planets to grow larger. Meteor impacts were so intense that Earth became molten. Iron, which is heavier than most other elements, sank to the center where it formed Earth's core.

4,400 mya: The Great Rain. When there were only a few meteors still crashing into it, Earth cooled down and formed a hard crust out of the lighter elements that floated to the surface. Earth's atmosphere cooled down too, which caused hydrogen and oxygen in the air to combine into water. Torrential rains covered Earth with oceans.

The Archean Eon—Bacteria Rule: 4,000 to 2,000 million years ago

Millions of Years Ago

4,600   4,000   3,000   2,000   1,000   500

Molten Earth   *Bacteria*   *Oxygen Crisis*

4,000 mya: Life begins. The first form of "life" may have been RNA (ribonucleic acid) molecules carrying genetic information that could reproduce themselves. They didn't have a membrane.

4,000 mya: The Rise of Bacteria. Hydrogen, made in the Big Bang, and five other elements made inside of stars—carbon, nitrogen, oxygen, phosphorus, and sulfur—were present in the early Earth. They are the six common elements for all of life. The very first single cell life probably began near hot sea vents, where they lived on hydrogen in gas

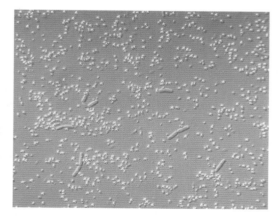

These rod and egg-shaped bacteria live in oceans, ponds, mud puddles—wherever there's water, you'll find them. Bacteria are Earth's recyclers. They digest dead plants, animals, and fungi, making nutrients available for other living things.

bubbles. They were archaebacteria ("ancient bacteria"). Another kind, called eubacteria—commonly just known as bacteria—multiplied into many different species. A bacterial cell does not have a nucleus. Their DNA floats loosely around inside the cell. Bacteria can trade DNA with each other throughout their entire lives. All living things use DNA (deoxyribonucleic acid) as the genetic code system—invented by bacteria—for guiding them in how to live. Bacteria reproduce themselves by splitting apart in a process called mitosis. They easily adapt to new environments because they can quickly share genetic information. That's why they can become resistant to drugs. Plants and animals cannot trade DNA.

3,700 mya: Photosynthesis—Earth plugs into the Sun. An early form of bacteria began to use sunlight energy to create food out of chemicals through photosynthesis. They were the ancestors of plants. Hydrogen was one of the primary foods of bacteria. Those who were better able to get hydrogen multiplied more than those who were not.

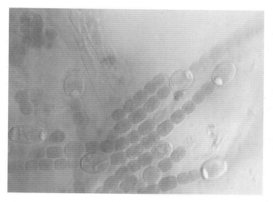

In some cyanobacteria colonies such as this one, the larger yellowish bacteria fix nitrogen while the green cells are the photosynthesizers. Cyanobacteria similar to these built stromatolites, or bacteria mounds, over 3,500 million years ago and they continue to build them today.

At first, photosynthesizing bacteria got hydrogen from gas bubbles. Later, another form of bacteria used photosynthesis to get hydrogen away from oxygen in water. They were cyanobacteria. Some cyanobacteria lived (and still live) in colonies. The colonies were so complex that cells had specialized jobs. Every time cyanobacteria pried hydrogen away from oxygen in water (H_2O), the oxygen atom turned into a gas and was released into the atmosphere. Oxygen was poison to most early life.

2,800 mya: Oxygen crisis—the first massive extinction. It started slowly, then turned into a full blown catastrophe. By 1,900 mya, Earth's atmospheric oxygen level rose so high that it killed almost all early life. But the crisis simultaneously presented an opportunity. The atmosphere's oxygen level stabilized at 21 percent, creating an ozone shield that would protect more complex forms of life from the Sun's damaging ultraviolet radiation. Without the oxygen crisis, more complex life, like you and the apple you ate for lunch, could not have evolved.

2,600 mya Bacteria get things ready on land. With their incredible powers to adapt quickly to new environments, bacteria were the first to move up on land. Over millions of years, they digested rock, turning it into soil, preparing the way for other life forms.

The Proterozoic Eon—Eukaryotes Join Bacteria: 2,000 to 540 million years ago

2,000 mya: Predators begin to prowl. Scientists don't know when the first single cell predators began to eat other living things. But it would have certainly started before 2,000 mya and was a crucial innovation that opened the way for more complex life. Predators cannot take their food directly out of rocks, air, water or sunlight. They have to eat other living things that can. Single cell predators are the ancestors of animals.

2,000 mya: Eukaryotes pack DNA into a nucleus. Probably in response to the oxygen crisis, a new kind of creature evolved—the eukaryote. It may have formed when an archaebacteria and a eubacteria merged into one and packed their DNA into a protective nucleus with a membrane. Many early eukaryotes were single cells, some lived only in groups, and still others could live either in groups or independently.

2,000 to 1,900 mya: Eukaryotes and mitochondria team up. Mitochondria, a kind of bacteria, weren't poisoned by oxygen. In fact, they became the powerhouses for eukaryotes by using oxygen to turn food molecules into energy that cells can use. In return, the eukaryote protected mitochondria from predators. Since then,

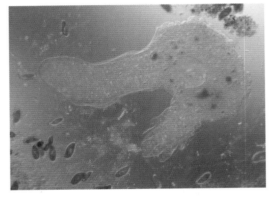

This amoeba, a single cell eukaryote, is similar to the very first eukaryotes. The nucleus appears as a large clear circle in the middle of the cell. It's feeding on bacteria and larger cells of algae.

mitochondria no longer live independently. Mitochondria live inside every single plant and animal cell, making it possible to live in Earth's oxygen atmosphere. With the eukaryote's DNA contained inside a protective nucleus, mitochondria could live inside eukaryote cells without damaging their DNA. In the same way that eukaryotes engulfed respiring mitochondria, some eukaryotes engulfed photosynthesizing bacteria and became algae. Algae later evolved into plants.

1,500 mya: Eukaryotes develop sex and death follows. Eukaryotes divide themselves into new cells containing half the number of chromosomes (gene-bearing structures) as there were before the split, a process called meiosis. This innovation led to the development of an egg from the female and a sperm from the male. When egg and sperm merge, the original number of chromosomes is restored. The new organism has a unique set of genes. This kind of reproduction opened the way for many different kinds of life. Around the same time that sex was developed, a new kind of death came into being. Up until that time, death was caused only by external factors—such as

extreme temperatures, predators, or starvation. Bacteria can live forever if no external forces cause them to die. They are immortal. But with the coming of sex, a new kind of death was internally programmed, a planned suicide called "apoptosis." Apoptosis is particularly important in the development of an embryo. For example, a human fetus has webbed fingers, like a duck, until the cells between the fingers die, allowing the fingers to separate. With sex and apoptosis, multi-cellular life can become more complex.

700 mya: Teaming up in the Garden of Ediacara. Eukaryotes began to form colonies of soft-bodied beings. They weren't plants or animals and they had no hard parts such as bones or skeletons. They were actually colonies of thousands of individual cells living and working together. Groups of cells specialized by taking on different jobs for the entire colony. Some took care of food intake; others took care of disposal. Scientists sometimes call this remarkable period the Garden of Ediacara,' named after the place in Australia where fossils for these creatures were found. The first soft-bodied animals appeared during this time. Mysteriously, most of the Ediacaran creatures disappeared.

The Phanerozoic Eon— Plants, Fungi, and Animals Join Bacteria and Early Eukaryotes: 540 million years ago to the present

Paleozoic Era—animals and plants arise: 540 to 245 million years ago

This two-inch long lancelet lives mostly buried in sand where it filters food out of water that flows into its mouth. It is very similar to the earliest ancestor of all animals with backbones, including fish and humans.

540 mya: Animals diversify. Soft-bodied animals first appeared during the Garden of Ediacara. Then, Earth began to experiment wildly with diverse body designs, laying down the plans for most of the major animal groups during what scientists call the "Cambrian Explosion." Animals are multi-cellular eukaryotes because their cells have nuclei. The first hard body parts appeared such as the exoskeleton in trilobites. Eyes were developed many times over in different species. Trilobites were among the first to develop eyes. The lenses were made out of transparent crystals of calcite backed by photosynthetic bacteria that sent messages to the trilobite's brain. Jellyfish developed the first muscles in their twitching tentacles. Descended from worms, lancelets evolved a "notochord" that would one day evolve into the backbone.

500 mya: Plants and fungi on the move. Plants and fungi evolved around the same time. Plants evolved from algae that hardened its outside so it could live on land without drying out. Through photosynthesis, plants obtained carbon. Fungi, living in soil, absorbed nitrogen from organic matter and made it available to plants through their roots. In a symbiotic relationship, they traded carbon and nitrogen with each other. Their partnership enabled them to spread across land. Plants and fungi are multi-cellular eukaryotes because their cells have nuclei.

450 mya: Insects take to the skies. Arthropods, such as spiders and insects, have a skeleton on the outside called an exoskeleton. They were the first animals on land. Today, they make up over 80% of the species in the animal kingdom.

400 mya: Amphibians come on land. Fresh water amphibians were the first vertebrates to develop legs to adapt to the harsh conditions on land. They developed a different kind of ear that could pick up sound traveling through air. Amphibians have to return to water to keep their skin moist and to lay their eggs, which do not have a protective shell.

340 mya: Reptiles dry off. Descended from amphibians, reptiles developed several crucial innovations enabling them to leave water permanently and move inland: (1) a closed egg with a protective shell and a yolk that supplied food to the growing embryo; (2) scaly waterproof skins that kept them from drying out; and (3) a penis for internal fertilization so they could breed on land.

Mesozoic Era—the age of dinosaurs: 245 to 65 million years ago

245 mya: Pangaea and the Permian Extinction. Continents, riding on top of tectonic plates, moved across thousands of miles to merge into one great landmass, called Pangaea. As they collided, shallow coastal seas disappeared—and then much of life disappeared too, in Earth's worst extinction. Was this extinction caused by the formation of Pangaea, a meteor crashing to Earth, or some other event? We do not know. Over 95% of all species disappeared, roughly twice as many as any of the other four mass extinctions that happened between 440 mya and today. Trilobites, Earth's most abundant marine animal for 300 million years, perished. Dog-sized reptiles, ancestors to mammals, were among the few reptiles to survive. Among the other surviving reptiles were the ancestors to a new ruling reptile that was about to take center stage.

225 mya: Out of reptiles—dinosaurs and mammals. Dinosaur and mammal lineages began to diverge with differences in skull shape and dental design. Both developed an upright stance with legs directly below their bodies, unlike reptiles before them who splayed their legs out to the side. Mammals developed other technologies that turned out to be crucial to their survival. Unlike cold-blooded animals that have to rely on heat from their environment for energy, mammals are warm-blooded. Even at night, they have energy to hunt for food—a crucial capability during the long night to come at the end of the age of dinosaurs. Mammals developed hair that helped them to stay warm. Mammals nurse their young, a characteristic that makes them different from other animals.

145 mya: Birds—dinosaurs who wouldn't quit. Archeopteryx, half dinosaur and half bird, had the same pelvic structure as dinosaurs and was probably descended from a chicken-sized dinosaur like Compsognathus. Like mammals, birds are warm-blooded. This single innovation may have helped save them from extinction.

Beetles, like all arthropods, have skeletons on the outside of their bodies. Beetles were among the first insects to pollinate flowers. Weevils, such as the one pictured here, are members of the largest family of beetles. Bees evolved much later.

110 mya: Earth blooms with flowers. The first flowering plants spread across Earth with the development of the encased seed. Just as reptiles and their descendants laid protected eggs with a yolk to feed the embryo, flowering plants produced enclosed seeds packed with food for the young plant. Of the 290,000 species of flowering plants today, only 20,000 can spread their pollen by wind or water. All the rest depend on animals to pollinate them. Flowering plants and animals evolved together in an intimate partnership: flowers providing nectar and fruit to animals, while animals spread pollen and seeds for plants.

65 mya: The sky falls and dinosaurs perish. The extinction of dinosaurs was probably caused by an asteroid crashing to Earth. A huge asteroid, 6 miles (10 km) wide, slammed into the Yucatan Peninsula in Mexico at 40,000 miles per hour (64,400 km/hr) with a force of 100 million single-megaton H-bombs. It penetrated the Earth's crust, sending dust into the atmosphere, increasing volcanic activity, starting global forest fires, and poisoning the air. Dust in the atmosphere blocked sunlight for months, or maybe even years, stopping photosynthesis and sending Earth into a deep freeze. Plants died, plant eaters died, then those who depended on the plant eaters died. One of the most important pieces of evidence supporting this theory is a thin layer of iridium found worldwide precisely at the sequence in rock from 65 million years ago. Iridium is rare on Earth but common in asteroids and meteorites. The theory is that a thin layer of iridium dust from the asteroid impact settled over Earth. Most animals weighing more than 55 pounds perished. All dinosaurs became extinct. Birds are the only descendents of dinosaurs alive today.

This opossum is very similar to the Alphadon, a primitive marsupial that survived during the massive extinction when all dinosaurs died.

The Five Kingdoms of Life

The kingdoms are divided into two major groups: *prokaryotes* and *eukaryotes*. Prokaryotes do not have nuclei; eukaryotes do. Bacteria are prokaryotes. All other living things are eukaryotes.

The Bacteria Kingdom: There are two kinds of bacteria, *archaebacteria* and *eubacteria*. Archaebacteria, probably the first form of life, evolved near hot sea vents. Eubacteria invented photosynthesis, respiration, and most other metabolisms. They continue to live almost everywhere, including inside of more complex life forms such as plants and animals. Descended from free-living eubacteria are chloroplasts (for photosynthesis in plants) and mitochondria (for respiration in plants and animals). Bacteria can transfer DNA to others throughout their lives. They reproduce by simple cell division, or mitosis. For two billion years, bacteria were the only form of life. They get their energy from chemicals, sunlight, or other living things. Some scientists split the two kinds of bacteria into two kingdoms for a total of six kingdoms. Other scientists keep them in one kingdom because they have the same kind of cell and swap genes with each other.

The Protoctista Kingdom: These were the first eukaryotes. They all live in water and include amoebas, algae, seaweeds and many others. They developed two-parent sexual reproduction and the capacity to form multi-cellular colonies that evolved into plants, fungi and animals. Protoctists get their energy from sunlight or other living things.

The Fungi Kingdom: This kingdom includes yeasts, molds and mushrooms. They absorb minerals and nutrients from organic matter. They are not plants; they don't photosynthesize. Mycorrhizal fungi have a symbiotic relationship with plants. They live on (and in) plant roots, absorb nitrogen out of soil and trade it for carbon with the plant. Many kinds of fungi are decomposers and crucial to forest ecologies. Molds and yeasts are used to make cheese, beer, and antibiotics such as penicillin.

The Plant Kingdom: Plants are multi-cellular eukaryotes whose cells contain chlorophyll for photosynthesis. They capture energy from the sun and use it to convert carbon dioxide and water into complex organic compounds and release oxygen. Oxygen released by plants is used by animals.

The Animal Kingdom: Animals are multi-cellular eukaryotes that eat other living things. They develop from the fertilization of a large egg by a small swimming sperm. Animals are different from other kingdoms in the way an animal embryo forms, the complexity of their organ systems, and their great capacity for movement.

Stories of Evolution that Inspired this Story

How did our universe, in all its majesty, come to be what it is today? Why is life so diverse? So complex? Humans have wrestled with these questions for thousands of years. You can imagine our ancestors, long, long ago, huddled around campfires on cold nights, telling stories to understand these great mysteries. All over the world, people told creation stories that came straight from their hearts and dreams. Some of these very same stories continue to nourish us today.

For over 500 years, humans have been telling science stories. Science stories are based on evidence. They are tested over and over to see if they match and predict what happens in the natural world. When a science story, or theory, doesn't match the natural world, the theory is changed or completely thrown away.

Scientists have been working on a theory of evolution for almost 200 years. A major breakthrough happened when **Charles Darwin** published his landmark book, *On the Origin of Species,* in 1859. He said that all life descended from a common ancestor. Different species came about through random variation and natural selection. Living things with variations that better adapted them to the environment, survived to pass their characteristics on to the next generation. Those less well adapted did not survive. Over a long time, slight variations added up to big differences, so big that new species came into being.

After Darwin died, scientists discovered that genes were the transmitters of characteristics to the next generation. With that discovery, Darwin's theory was confirmed and amplified as Neo-Darwinism. But many scientists wondered whether random variation and natural selection explained everything about the great diversity of life.

Can living things make choices that lead to evolutionary change? **Thomas Berry** and **Brian Swimme**, in *The Universe Story* (1994), say yes, they can. For example, land ancestors of whales "chose" to return to the sea. Then, over many generations, through random variation and natural selection, the sea environment shaped whales into the form we know today. Berry and Swimme summarized the shaping powers of evolution as chance, choice and necessity; that is, genetic variation, niche creation, and natural selection. Genetic variation arises by chance; niche creation occurs when living things choose a new environment, and natural selection sculpts new species by favoring those that adapt to the environment.

Evolutionary biologist **Lynn Margulis**, in her book *Acquiring Genomes: A Theory of the Origins of Species* (2002), says that symbiosis brings about far more significant change than random variation. Two species living in a symbiotic relationship can form a third species. For example, algae and fungi merged into lichen. Symbiosis brings about a bigger change, she said, because it introduces not a single change to a single gene, but introduces a whole new set of genes.

James Lovelock and **Lynn Margulis** developed the Gaia hypothesis in 1974. Evidence shows, they say, that Earth's rock, water, air and life are interacting in ways that keep the planet suitable for life. Earth, as a whole, sustains life in a process we call evolution. How can this be? Is Earth alive? There's so much for us to discover. Can science answer all our questions?

Elisabet Sahtouris and Willis Harmon, authors of *Biology Revisioned* (2000), proposed that consciousness existed first, then "poured itself" into an intelligent self-organizing universe. In this paradigm, evolution has direction and is not accidental. This view is reflected in India's ancient Vedic tradition and in many of the stories told by our ancient ancestors. Most scientists say that this perspective cannot be tested and therefore falls outside the realm of science.

How will future discoveries change our stories? Whatever we find out, when the sun goes down and stars begin to emerge in the dark night, we will share our stories, as we always have, gathered around a campfire.

Glossary

Animals Multi-cellular eukaryote that develops from a hollow ball of cells (an embryonic blastula).

Apoptosis Internally programmed cell death that allows cells to self-destruct. This innovation is critically important for shaping embryos.

Amphibians Vertebrates that live in water and on land. They must lay their eggs in water.

Bacteria Microscopic prokaryote.

Birds Warm-blooded, two-legged, egg-laying vertebrates with feathers and wings. Birds are descended from dinosaurs.

Chromosomes Structures in cells that carry genes.

Dinosaurs A large group of extinct, mostly land-dwelling, four-limbed reptiles of the Mesozoic Era.

Eukaryote Single cell and multi-cellular organisms whose cells have nuclei.

Evolution In biology, change in organisms over generations.

Fungi (singular: fungus) Multi-cellular eukaryotes such as yeasts, molds, and mushrooms that live off organic matter.

Gaia hypothesis The idea that Earth's rock, water, air and life are interacting with each other in ways that keep the planet suitable for life. In doing so, the Earth behaves in a way similar to how a living organism behaves.

Genes Unit of hereditary information on a chromosome.

Genome The complete genetic material of an organism.

Insects Small animals with an exoskeleton and segmented body, such as beetles, bees, flies, and mosquitoes.

Mammals Vertebrate animal giving birth to live young and nurturing them on milk.

Meiosis Cell division that results in offspring cells with half the number of chromosomes as the parent cell.

Mitochondria The part in a eukaryote cell that descended from free-living respiring bacteria. They use oxygen to convert food molecules into energy.

Mitosis Cell division that results in offspring cells with the same number of chromosomes as the parent cell.

Natural selection The subtractive environmental force that causes the survival and reproduction of some individuals instead of others. Generation by generation, the better-adapted lines survive to pass on features that give them an advantage in local environments.

Plants Multi-cellular eukaryotes that can photosynthesize.

Photosynthesis A process that transforms light energy into chemical energy.

Prokaryote A microscopic organism that does not have a nucleus. Bacteria are prokaryotes.

Protoctist Earliest eukaryotes, they live independently or in colonies. All living things other than plants, animals, fungi, and bacteria are protoctists (lit: "first being").

Reptiles Class of air-breathing, generally scaly, vertebrates that includes snakes, lizards, alligators, and dinosaurs.

Seaweed Colonial marine alga in the Protoctist Kingdom.

Sex Combining genes from more than one source to form a new single being.

Symbiosis Intimate physical partnership between two different kinds of organisms that lasts over a long time.

Vertebrates Animals that have a backbone or spinal column including all mammals, fishes, birds, reptiles and amphibians.

Resources

Books for Children and Teachers

All I See is Part of Me by Chara Curtis (1989). A child recognizes her connection to everything. (Ages 1 to 8)

Earth Dance by Joanne Ryder (1996). Guides the child in imagining that they are the Earth. (Ages 4 to 12)

Earth Story by Eric Maddern, illustrated by Leo Duff (1988). A magically-told story about Earth's formation.

Everybody Needs a Rock by Byrd Baylor (1974). Rules about appreciating a very special rock. (Ages 3 to 7)

Guide to Dinosaurs: A Thrilling Journey through Prehistoric Times by David Lambert (2000). A great dinosaur book with incredible pictures. (All ages)

Life Without Light: A Journey to Earth's Dark Ecosystems by M. Stewart (1999). A science book about life that survives without light. (Ages 9 to 13)

Happy Birthday Universe! A Cosmic Curriculum for Children by Kym Farmer (1993). Available through www.sycamorehollow.com. An excellent curriculum for K to 6th grade.

On the Day You Were Born by Debra Frasier (1991). The community of life welcomes a child. (Ages 1 to 8)

Books for Adults

Acquiring Genomes: A Theory of the Origins of Species by Lynn Margulis and Dorian Sagan (2002). Very important book about the role of symbiosis in evolution.

A Walk Through Time by Sidney Liebes, Elisabet Sahtouris, and Brian Swimme (1998). A great presentation of the Earth story with stunning photographs.

Biology Revisioned by Elisabet Sahtouris and Willis Harmon (2000). A different view of biology with consciousness as life's origin.

Conscious Evolution by Barbara Marx Hubbard (1998). Places the current global situation inside the story of evolution.

Cradle of Life by J. William Schopf (1999). A fascinating scientific inquiry into the origin of life.

EarthSpirit: A Handbook for Nurturing an Ecological Christianity by Michael Dowd (1991). The first book to popularize evolution for Christians.

Evolution: The Triumph of an Idea by Carl Zimmer (2001). Companion to the PBS series. (See "Other Resources, below.)

Dinosaurs and Prehistoric Animals by Dougal Dixon, Barry Cox, R.J.G. Savage and Brian Gardiner (1988). Detailed information and pictures.

Five Kingdoms: An Illustrated Guide to the Phyla of Life on Earth by Lynn Margulis and K.V. Schwartz (3rd ed., 1998).

Green Space, Green Time: The Way of Science by Connie Barlow (1997). A controversial book about breaching the barrier between science and meaning.

Life: A Natural History of the First Four Billion Years of Life on Earth by Richard Fortey (1998). A very readable comprehensive survey supplemented by stories about scientists.

Microcosmos: Four Billion Years of Microbial Evolution by Lynn Margulis and Dorion Sagan (1986). A classic.

One River, Many Wells by Matthew Fox (2001). Celebrates the teachings that all spiritual traditions hold in common and the science underlying a new creation story.

The Book of Life: An Illustrated History of the Evolution of Life on Earth edited by Stephen Jay Gould (1993). A great resource book with lots of illustrations, charts, and maps.

The Dream of the Earth by Thomas Berry (1988). A very important collection of essays that discuss the primary role of Earth.

The Great Work by Thomas Berry (1999). Lays out the need to reorient our culture and institutions to the Earth community as a whole.

The Sacred Depths of Nature by Ursula Goodenough (1998). Poetically discusses modern scientific understanding and spiritual yearnings.

The Universe Story: From the Primordial Flaring Forth to the Ecozoic Era, A Celebration of the Unfolding of the Cosmos by Brian Swimme and Thomas Berry (1994). A classic that explores both inner and outer dimensions.

The Universe is a Green Dragon by Brian Swimme (2001). An eloquent discussion about the dynamics of the universe.

The Web of Life by Fritjof Capra (1996). A brilliant and accessible synthesis of complexity theory, Gaia theory, and several others.

Videos

Canticle to the Cosmos with Brian Swimme (1995).

Earth's Imagination with Brian Swimme (1998).

Life on Earth with David Attenborough (1978).

Looking at Microbes with L Olendzenski, S. Goodwin and L. Margulis (1998).

Microcosmos Videos with A. Weir and L. Margulis (1999).

Other Resources

BioMedia (www.eBioMEDIA.com). A website with great closeup pictures of microbes and other life.

Five Kingdoms: A multimedia guide to the phyla of life on Earth (2nd ed., CD-ROM, 2002). Available through Biodiversity Center of ETI, Multimedia Interactive Software, Amsterdam, The Netherlands.

Life Web: Biophilosophy (www.ratical.org/LifeWeb). Website for articles, videos and books by Elisabet Sahtouris.

The Great Story (www.thegreatstory.org). A website by Michael Dowd and Connie Barlow with a detailed timeline, articles, parables, and ritual celebrations for telling the story of the universe.

PBS website (www.pbs.org/evolution), Contains a wealth of information about Darwin, evolution.

Mary Ellen Hill (mehstories@citycom.com) is a professional storyteller in the San Francisco area whose specialty is "We Are The Stars That Sing: The Story Of The Universe."

Jennifer Morgan, author of this book, tells stories for children and adults, provides teacher training, and leads adult workshops. www.UniverseStories.com

Jennifer Morgan's work as a storyteller, author, educator and environmental advocate flows out of her love of the natural world and cosmology. As former director of the Northeast Organic Farming Association of New Jersey, she started numerous educational and marketing programs for farmers and consumers, both locally and nationally. Currently she is an adjunct staff member at Genesis Farm, teaching the Sacred Universe Story. A portion of Ms. Morgan's royalties from the sale of this book are donated to Earth literacy centers. Her storytelling evolved from bedtime stories for her son who wanted to know more and more, even the texture of the edge of the Universe. She believes that our cosmology stories fundamentally shape us—our relationships, our work, our play, our culture, our institutions, our everything. She can be contacted at www.UniverseStories.com.

Dana Lynne Andersen, M.A., is a multi-media artist, playwright and teacher with degrees in philosophy and consciousness studies. Her paintings, often very large in size, explore the swirling forces of energy that underlie matter and seek to reveal life's numinous mystery. She believes that as our "depth perception" expands—billions of galaxies discovered in our lifetime!—it is also essential to expand perception inwardly to the vastness within. She is founder of Awakening Arts, a network of artists who "affirm the noble purpose of art as a vehicle for uplifting the human spirit." Posters of the art in this book are available from awakeningarts.com.

Author's Acknowledgments

Many incredible Earthlings created this story. To create such stunning illustrations, Dana Andersen lived and slept in paint for over nine months. Miriam MacGillis and the Genesis Farm staff, who started me on this writing adventure, continued to guide me. Thomas Berry, Ph.D., continued to lure me into deeper understandings. Emily Case, M.Ed., steered me around many biology boulders, taking panic calls at all times, even Saturday night. Mark Henry, Ph.D., researched many questions and gave storytelling suggestions. Princeton professors Drs. Stephen Pacala, Henry Horn, and David Stern, generously gave precious time and lent piles of books. David Parris, Ph.D., Curator of Natural History, New Jersey State Museum, provided dinosaur information through fascinating tales. Connie Barlow, Ph.D., and Rev. Michael Dowd supplied inspiration and information. Jean and Larry Edwards, gave encouragement and more pieces for the puzzle. Herb Simmens served up many a burrito with brainstorming. Other members of my Epic of Evolution group—Ralph Copleman, Maria Myers, Bob Wallace, Susan Curry, Mary Coelho, Ph.D., and Andy Smith—were my local incubator. The Princeton Public Library was my office; the librarians my advisers at the ready. Emily and Kori Bloom mulled the story for hours on a hot August day. Princeton Charter School voted on the cover. Co-creators of all ages joined into the fray. To name a few: Jeremy Taylor, Charles Marsee, Patricia Gordon, Max Tech-Czarny, Corinne Egner, Dudley Beach, Susan Jefferies, Soren Rasmussen, Victoria Monaco, Laura Langfeld, Karen Chaffee, Theresa Brown, Ph.D., Arthur Kosowsky, Ph.D., Cynthia Cordes, and Helene van Rossum. Morgan family storytelling by the campfire—with Maureen, John, Douglas, Frissie, Seth, Lael, Brian, Adele, Mike, and Willard—was an enormous help. I am so deeply grateful to Muffy Weaver and Glenn Hovemann of Dawn Publications, for birthing another very challenging book. I can't imagine working with any other publisher. My son Morgan Martindell, now twelve, still carries the mantle of chief first-cut editor. Special thanks go to the Lyme spirochetes who kept him home from school when final revisions were being made. Cleo and Milo, our dear cats, curled up by the computer to lend their support too. And most of all, you, dear Universe, our source and our destiny, you are the ultimate writer, painter, and brainstormer who brought this book into being. Thank you, thank you!

Dawn Publications offers children's books that encourage an appreciation for the web of life on Earth.

Also by Jennifer Morgan: *Born With a Bang: The Universe Tells Our Cosmic Story.* The first in the Universe series tells the story of life from the very beginning to the creation of planet Earth. Winner of The Teacher's Choice Award.

Girls Who Looked Under Rocks, by Jeannine Atkins. Six girls, from the 17th to the 20th century, didn't run from spiders or snakes but crouched down to take a closer look. They became pioneering naturalists, passionate scientists, and energetic writers or artists.

John Muir: My Life with Nature, by Joseph Cornell. John Muir's joyous enthusiasm for nature is contagious in this telling, mostly in his own words, of his remarkable adventures with nature.

Stickeen: John Muir and the Brave Little Dog by John Muir as retold by Donnell Rubay. In this classic true story, the relationship between the great naturalist and a small dog is changed forever by their adventure on a glacier in Alaska.

Under One Rock: Bugs, Slugs and other Ughs by Anthony Fredericks. No child will be able to resist looking under a rock after reading this rhythmic, engaging story.

A Tree in the Ancient Forest, by Carol Reed-Jones, demonstrates how interdependent are the plants and animals around a grand old fir.

This is the Sea that Feeds Us, by Robert F. Baldwin. In simple cumulative verse, this book explores the oceans' fabulous food web that reaches all the way from plankton to people.

Salmon Stream, by Carol Reed-Jones, follows the life cycle of salmon, who hatch in a stream, travel the world, and return to their birthplace against staggering odds.

Saguaro Moon, A Desert Journal by Kristin Joy Pratt. This young author-illustrator's latest book is a model nature journal on the desert habitat. Kristin is the teenage "Eco-star" made famous by her earlier books, *A Walk in the Rainforest, A Swim through the Sea,* and *A Fly in the Sky.*

Three books by J. Patrick Lewis, *Earth & You—A Closer View; Earth & Us—Continuous;* and *Earth & Me—Our Family Tree,* introduce the major habitats, the continuity of life and the connections between animals and their environment.

Do Animals Have Feelings, Too? by David Rice presents fascinating true stories of animal behavior, and then asks the reader whether they think the animal is acting on the basis of feelings or just instinctively.

Dawn Publications is dedicated to inspiring in children a deeper understanding and appreciation for all life on Earth. To view our full list of titles, or to order, please visit our web site at www.dawnpub.com, or call 800-545-7475.